Ever had a parent or teacher lecture you about how important it is to wash your hands? It might surprise you to learn that many folks around the world struggle to make sure their families have something as simple as soap or shampoo, and that can lead to all sorts of health problems. Everyone deserves the chance to keep clean, so that's why I'm so excited to share the story of Lewis partnering with Homewood Suites and Clean the World®. I hope you enjoy… and remember to always wash your hands!

"**O**ww owwww owww owww ow!" squawked Lewis the duck as he tried to wipe soapy suds out of his eyes. He was grabbing a quick shower after arriving to his favorite home-away-from-home, Homewood Suites by Hilton. He had flown into Duck City that morning for the annual Duck, Inc. International Conference and was thrilled to learn that his favorite hotel was right across the street from the event!

B

eing away from home is hard, but Lewis appreciated all the friendly faces and homey touches at Homewood Suites. "Welcome, Mr. Duck!" greeted Jenn, the front desk agent. "Enjoy your stay."

The next morning on his way to breakfast, a poster in the elevator caught his eye. It was about a special program called Clean the World®, and Lewis made a note to ask about it later.

"**I**'m glad you asked, Lewis!" smiled Amy, the General Manager. "As you know, proper hand-washing and hygiene helps keep you and those around you from getting sick. We partner with Clean the World to supply recycled soap to people in need all over the world. Let me show you how it works…"

"Here at Homewood Suites, our housekeepers collect used soaps and other products from the rooms they clean," explained Amy. "They take any bar of soap, even if it's teensy-weensy and almost used up." "That's not very much soap," laughed Lewis. "You'd be surprised," replied Amy.

"This is where we store the soap we've collected," said Amy in the suite-keeping office. "The green bin is for soap bars; the blue one's for used shampoo bottles. Once the bins fill up, we notify Clean the World, and they have them made into brand new bars of soap." Lewis had to see that to believe it.

At the Clean the World facility, Amy and Lewis met with Shawn, the person who started the organization. "Soap recycling is a fascinating process, Lewis," said Shawn. "Let me show you what we do once a shipment of used soap arrives."

Shawn led Amy and Lewis to a sorting area where volunteers were separating soap bars and shampoo bottles. "Wow," exclaimed Lewis. "I can't believe there's so much extra soap and shampoo!"

"Soap noodles?" said a surprised Lewis. "That's right," explain[ed] Shawn. "We take the sorted bars and clean them to make sure any leftover germ[s] are gone and then cut the bars into noodles to prepare them for melting." Lewi[s] was going to have trouble the next time he was served spaghetti…

Lewis was truly amazed by it all. Who knew it was even possible to recycle used soap? A big machine turned the melted soap into a large bar that could be cut up into smaller bars. "Old soap yesterday," smiled Shawn. "New soap today!"

"So what happens next?" asked Lewis. "Good question," said Shawn. "Once the soap is made, it's boxed up and loaded onto our Clean the World truck. Then it's ready to go wherever it's needed. We're actually getting ready to take this batch to Guatemala. Care to join us?"

retty soon, Lewis and his family boarded the plane for Guatemala. The plan was for Shawn, Jim, and the rest of their team to help give out soap in remote villages. They even met up with the Chief Executive Officer (CEO) of Hilton – Chris – and everyone had a great time giving soap to the locals. It made Lewis feel good to know he was helping folks be able to stay clean.

Back at his office at Duck, Inc., Lewis was washing his wings and reflecting on all the things he had learned about the soap recycling process and how it really made a difference in the world. Lewis knew that little things can be very important, and Clean the World had taught him that a simple used bar of soap can change lives for the better.

ow long should it take to wash your hands? Here's a song Lewis uses to help him remember. Make sure you sing the song twice to get your hands nice and clean!

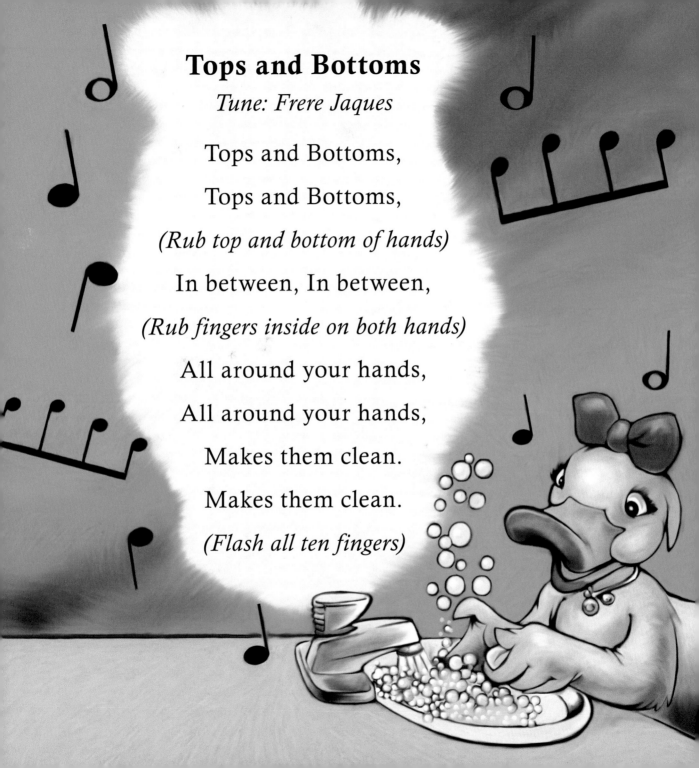

Tops and Bottoms

Tune: Frere Jaques

Tops and Bottoms,

Tops and Bottoms,

(Rub top and bottom of hands)

In between, In between,

(Rub fingers inside on both hands)

All around your hands,

All around your hands,

Makes them clean.

Makes them clean.

(Flash all ten fingers)

Clean the World
has a two-part mission:

• Collect and recycle soap and hygiene products discarded every day by the hospitality industry and other sectors that generate environmental waste.

• Through the distribution of these and other donated products to impoverished people, prevent millions of hygiene-related deaths each year, reduce the morbidity rate for hygiene-related illnesses and encourage vigorous childhood development.

Learn more at **cleantheworld.org**

Author Bio:

Christian Duncan is an avid duck admirer who lives with his three dogs, Seth, Mary Margret and Barnabas in Memphis, TN. A graduate of Mississippi State University, he got his literary start as co-author (with his father, Bill Duncan) of *Lewis the Duck Goes to Mexico*, *Lewis the Duck Lends a Helping Wing* and *Lewis the Duck Flies Around the World*. His first solo book was *Lewis the Duck Saves the Day*.

Illustrator Bio:

Greg Cravens is the creator of the syndicated cartoon, The Buckets. He enjoys spending time with his wife Paula and sons Gideon and Cory. He has illustrated *Lewis the Duck and His Long Trip*, *Lewis the Duck Goes to Canada*, *Lewis the Duck Goes to Mexico*, *Lewis the Duck Lends a Helping Wing*, *Lewis the Duck Flies Around the World*, *Lewis the Duck Saves The Day* and *Lewis the Duck Cleans Up The World*. He serves on the board of the National Cartoonists Society, which he has been a member of for twenty years.